• MEET •
CAROL HIGHSMITH

Read With You
Center for Excellence in STEAM Education

Read With You

Published by Read With You Publishing. Printed in the United States of America.

ISBN: 979-8-88618-501-0
First Edition September 2023

Howdy! I'm Carol Highsmith. I've visited every state in America to photograph small towns, big cities, and everything in between.

I donated my photographs to the Library of Congress so that Americans everywhere can learn about their country.

Visual Documentarian Carol M. Highsmith, Carbon County, Wyoming, 2016

I began taking photos in the 1980s, but I like to photograph buildings that were around long before I was born. Do you know what this wheel is for?

It's a gristmill. It uses the power of water to grind grain into flour for making bread or cake. This mill was built in 1864.

Dells Mill, Augusta, Wisconsin, 2016

Other places that I visit are much more modern. What do you think these rocks are part of?

I love architecture, or the way buildings are designed. I enjoy capturing both fancy and ordinary buildings.

A Rock-Garden Plaza, Truth or Consequences, New Mexico, 2021

When I get close to something to photograph it, that's called a *close-up* or a *detail shot*. What details do you notice here?

AIRBORNE
AA

These women are continuing the traditions of their Native American ancestors.

Members of the Native American Women Warriors, Colorado Springs, Colorado, 2015

Let's turn our gaze back to the land. Since I want to photograph life all over the United States, I take lots of pictures of nature, too.

This spot used to be a mining town. Big photos of the world around us, like this one, are called *landscapes*.

Scene at the Lake Valley Historic Site, Sierra County, New Mexico, 2021

The USA has a diverse population, and I enjoy photographing the people as well as the land. Can you guess what vehicle this man is driving?

He is part of a community that chooses to live without modern technology. What do you think it would be like to not have a TV or car?

An Amish or Mennonite Man and His Horse and Buggy, Washington County, Iowa, 2016

This event is one of the most famous events in the city of Philadelphia. People think it is the oldest continuing folk festival in the United States!

Look at all those colors. What would you wear to the Mummers Parade?

Mummers Parade on Broad Street, Philadelphia, Pennsylvania, 2019

The next time you travel, take a camera and keep an eye out for unique details and beautiful landscapes! You never know what you will discover.

Life in a Bubble Can Be Fun, Frisco, Colorado, 2016

Find Examples

This photograph is *An Elaborate Dragon-Themed Mailbox, East Haven, Vermont* (2017).

What makes this mailbox unique?

Why do you think Highsmith stopped to take a photo of this mailbox?

Which photo in the book do you think looks most like this one? Why?

This photo was taken shortly before Halloween. Does that change how you think about it?

Connect

This photograph is *The Majestic Peaks of the Teton Range, Grand Teton National Park, Wyoming* (2015).

Have you ever been somewhere like this? Where was it?

If you were a photographer, would you spend more time in nature or in cities? Why?

Where would you go to take the best possible photos of your country?

What might make it hard for a photographer to take a beautiful shot like this one?

Craft

Option 1

1. Walk slowly through your home with a camera or cellphone camera.

2. When you find something beautiful or unique, take a close-up shot of it.

3. Print the photos and label them with explanations of why you took each one.

Option 2

1. Search through this book and find your favorite photograph.

2. With the help of an adult, look up information about the place where it was taken.

3. Plan a trip to that state and write down what you would photograph if you went there.